TO MY FRIENDS,
ALPHONSE & ANNE,

MERRY CHRISTMAS 2016

[signature]

Wine COCKTAILS

50 Stylish Sippers that Show Off Your
Reds, Whites, and Rosés

A.J. RATHBUN

PHOTOGRAPHY BY MELISSA PUNCH

The Harvard Common Press
Boston, Massachusetts

FOR ALL THE PROFESSIONAL AND
HOME BARTENDERS WHO HAVE
INTRODUCED ME TO NEW DRINKS
(BOTH WITH WINE AND WITHOUT):
I'M IN YOUR DEBT FOREVER.

The Harvard Common Press
535 Albany Street, Boston, Massachusetts 02118
www.harvardcommonpress.com

Printed in China
Printed on acid-free paper

Library of Congress Cataloging-in-Publication Data
Rathbun, A. J. (Arthur John), 1969-
   Wine cocktails : 50 stylish sippers that show off your reds, whites, and rosés / A.J.
Rathbun.
      p. cm.
   Includes bibliographical references and index.
   ISBN 978-1-55832-407-7 (hardcover : alk. paper)
   1. Cocktails. 2. Wine and wine making. I. Title.
   TX951.R1755 2009
   641.8'74--dc22
                              2008035421

Special bulk-order discounts are available on this and other Harvard Common Press
books. Companies and organizations may purchase books for premiums or resale,
or may arrange a custom edition, by contacting the Marketing Director at the
address above.

Book design by Elizabeth Van Itallie
Photographs by Melissa Punch
Food and drink styling by Stephana Bottom
Prop styling by Loren Simons
Author photographs by Natalie Fuller

10 9 8 7 6 5 4 3 2 1

CONTENTS

ACKNOWLEDGMENTS

The wine universe, and the wine cocktail universe, is a large, wonderful, diverse place, one I've been lucky enough to spend a lot of time exploring. Even luckier is the fact that the time I've spent there has been shared with an array of fine folks, folks who helped me find my way into and around that universe and who made it a better place to be. While everyone I've had a wine cocktail with gets a big cheer from me, a few people deserve special thanks for the extra help they gave me during my wine cocktail adventures. First and foremost, thanks to Valerie Cimino, editor extraordinaire, who came up with the original idea for this book, and who then provided the direction and assistance needed to make it bubble and sing. Thanks also to Bruce Shaw and the many, many unbelievable people who work at The Harvard Common Press for their cheerful and right-on aid and support. HCPers rule! And you have my thanks forever. In addition, huge props to award-winning photographer Melissa Punch, who makes the drinks look so enticing and who's always a delight to work with, and to copyeditor Debra Hudak for her keen eye. All of you, the next bottle or round's on me.

And speaking of rounds I should buy, my agent Michael Bourret deserves many, because without his guidance, good taste, relentless support, and good cheer, I wouldn't even have been able to get the corkscrew out and start opening those bottles of wine, much less have started shaking and stirring and pouring them into tasty mixes. MB, again and again, thanks for being there for my questions, for helping round out my ideas, and most of all for being in my corner of the bar.

Thinking about people whom I'm blessed to be able to hang out with in a bar (or a backyard) while sipping a wine cocktail, a big thanks to those who tested, tasted, made suggestions, and provided liquid opinions during the writing of this book. I'm seriously charmed to have so many friends who fit into this group, and I hope you know that without you, making these drinks certainly wouldn't have been as much of a kick. There are a few specific folks who deserve their own bottle (or cask) of wine for their assistance, including Jeremy and Megan, Kyla and Mike, Mark and Leslie, Andrea (thanks for the Rosy Navel naming aid), Christi, Cash, my pal and drink-video-making-master Brad, mighty media trainers and pals Lisa Ekus and Sarah Baurle, the supportive Brad P., and my wonderful family near and far (especially my sister Holly, for spreading the Sangria legend around). Wandering within the wine cocktails wouldn't have been nearly as enjoyable without you.

Of course, the wine cocktails wouldn't flow, or the wine cocktail universe be worth visiting, without the continual help and support of one person, my wife, Natalie. Nat, thanks for smiling when the glassware overcame the cabinet space, and for not even batting an eye when the boxes and boxes of wine and liquors showed up, and for always being ready to taste a fresh drink. I'll chill a bottle of Prosecco and open a bottle of Aperol, you grab a couple of glasses, a lemon, and the Sookie dog, and we'll meet in five minutes in the backyard for another wonderful afternoon.

INTRODUCTION

The history of folks gathering to share a toast and a tasty beverage goes back so far as to be untraceable. Let's just say it's been a part of communal existence since gatherings were held in dimly lit caves and fashions tended toward the simple animal skin. Wine has been a part of this celebratory consumption for a good part of history, tracing its lineage back to the 6000 to 5000 BC range from all reports, and present in most cultures since then (from the gregarious Greeks to the rollicking Romans to the ever-loving Egyptians and most folks around before and after them). Wine is more a part of life and history than the car, the telephone, the computer, or any of the other devices so many seem to have a hard time living without. If you're living without a nice relationship with the vino, many throughout our shared human history might say you're not living at all.

But you might not know that mixing wine with other ingredients has long been a part of wine's history as well. First and foremost it was mixed with water, as many ancient cultures thought that drinking straight wine was not only dangerous but bad form. Ask Herodotus, who said that one Cleomenes "lost his senses" and died a horrific death from drinking unmixed wine. Wine was also mixed with fruits, spices, and even honey on occasion in our early history, both to use these ingredients as flavoring agents and to use wine as a preservative (naturally the wine was flavored in this usage as well). This practice in many places didn't change with the passing of time. In Europe, the practice of mixing wine with other ingredients to make scrumptious drinks never stopped—which is why you see a variety of modern wine cocktails in France and Italy. The move by these drinks to America has been a long time coming. There has been a resistance from those who think that their wine must be sipped solo. This is a crying shame (if I can get weepy for a second) because you, the drinking public, need to realize the greatness of the wine cocktail.

I can see some of you cringing right now. But stay with me for a bit, and see if I can bring you around (a little trust in your dedicated author, please). First off, it's not like this is a sparkling fresh idea that I'm unearthing like a giant spiritous jewel seeing the light of day for the first time. The classic cocktailians of history, who set down the earliest tomes of cocktail lore, were as a rule well versed in wine, and they stirred and shook combinations that can only be called wine cocktails. A number of the recipes in this very book are updated versions from older books. There's a scrumptious precedence it would be a mistake to ignore. Also, not to get all continental, but when visiting our European pals, there's no shaking of fingers at a tall drink that features both Prosecco and Aperol, for example, or fresh fruit and a sparkling Riesling. Why shouldn't everyone, worldwide, take advantage of these flavor minglings? I say we shouldn't hesitate.

We are in the midst of an ideal time if you like wine and cocktails. There are more and more varietals and varieties of wines available around the world, and more talented folks are taking the time to make excellent wine in all price ranges. At the same time, a vast assortment (expanding daily it seems) of liqueurs and liquors is available, not to mention fresh kiwis, mandarins, and other kinds of fruits, and a range of other mixers, enough to make a cocktail fanatic's head spin. This multinationalism of drinks cannot be ignored. Embrace wine cocktails, from beautiful bubblies to ravishing reds to wonderful whites to sweet sippers and entertaining exotics. You'll soon find yourself riding a Blue Wave, snuggling up to the Lamb's Wool, walking with Lord Charles, and slipping into a Tuxedo. That's the kind of company that lets you not only be a part of history, but also lets you host truly historical parties, festivities that are remembered long after the last drop. So let go of your preconceived notions and enter the world of wine cocktails. Once you learn more about it, you'll definitely want to visit—and you may never want to leave.

WINE COCKTAIL BASICS

I invite you to take a magical journey with me, to a realm many have yet to experience, a wonderful realm occupied by the Frisco, the Sake'd Saint, the Kitty, the Refroidisseur, and many other fantastic imbibables, a realm where the music is either jumping or slightly subdued (depending on your party mood), a realm where toasting is as common as fresh fruit juice, a realm where wine and liquor live together, a realm known as the world of wine cocktails.

Wait, you say, hold on just a minute. Before we go on this "magical journey," I have a simple question: What are wine cocktails, anyway? Well, they are just what they sound like: Wine cocktails are mixed drinks that include a type of wine as a major ingredient, whether it's red wine, white wine, sparkling wine, dessert wine, or one of wine's more international cousins, such as sake. And, as the drinks are always mixed in some way, that means that there must be something in our wine cocktails besides wine. The list of ingredients accompanying wine is vast, including liquors such as gin and brandy, liqueurs from all over the earth, such as Strega and Chambord, fresh juice, fresh fruit, herbs, and other traditional mixers like club soda.

Hold on one more sec, though, you say—I thought wine was something consumed on its own. Hasn't there been a recent wine explosion because people are sipping more wine? Wine is a wide category, and one that is deliciously fun to delve into. I'm not suggesting you should give up enjoying wine by itself (that would be a sacrilege). For that matter, I wouldn't turn down a nice glass if you offered it to me. And of course, one should always enjoy a higher-end vintage bottle on its own. But one of the lovely aspects of the wine cocktail is that it lets you use, and consume, wine in a wider range of situations, and lets you employ the flavors and notes of different types of wine in different drinks, blending them with other flavors. Of course, one of the other (and maybe more important) aspects of the wine cocktails in this book is that they taste so darn good—and wouldn't you be sad if you missed out due to some allegiance to only consuming wine solo?

To be accurate, wine cocktails have actually been around quite a long time. Champagne and sparkling wines fit into the wine cocktails realm, and the classic Champagne cocktail, with its simply brilliant mix of sugar, Angostura bitters, and the bubbly, has been around at least since the mid-1800s (it's in Jerry Thomas's *Bar-Tender's Guide or How to Mix Drinks* from 1862). While many find this pretty acceptable (due to Sunday-morning mimosas and the like), many would also be surprised to find out that at the same time, and during the cocktail heyday in the latter part of the last century, there were also many other drinks being made with red and white wine mixed with liquors, liqueurs, and other ingredients, just like the beverages in this book.

The question is now for you: Why wouldn't you slip in a nice wine cocktail at your next gala, backyard lawn-bowling tourney, or candlelit dinner for two? I strongly suggest it (and applaud it, if you invite me to such a celebration). More and more people are drinking wine on an everyday basis, as well as learning a bit more about wine and having access to a greater variety of wine. At the same time, cocktail love and culture are back on the rise, and people are enjoying good cocktails and good spirits with their friends more than ever. It's time to bring these two great trends together in one friendly, tasty place. The realm of wine cocktails is that place.

A Word or Two about Wine

The wine spectrum is enormous. With production happening all over the globe, and inventive and original winemakers and wineries popping up all the time, it can be daunting even walking into the wine aisle at the corner market. Luckily, there are books, thick and heavy books, that detail the ins and outs for you. But here, we're concerned with wine cocktails, and with getting to the drinking of said cocktails as soon as possible. With that in mind, I'm not going to detail every varietal of wine under the sun, but just lay out a few good ground rules that will help you navigate this book and end up with the finest wine-based drinks.

First, remember that recipes here feature wine mixed with some other ingredient. There are no wine cocktails that are solely wine. So, you'll always be modifying the wine's innate flavors. With that in mind, I suggest not using extraordinarily high-end wines. We all know that wine prices range from the very inexpensive to the extremely expensive. If you're someone who has a wine cellar packed with high-end wine, that's great. You should still try these wine cocktails (because you'll love them), but pick up some nice, mid-range wine to use in them. But don't go too low, either. If you switch in some Mad Dog 20/20, the wine cocktails won't sing; instead they'll squawk. You want good-quality wines, but wines you won't feel bad about mixing later. We don't want any wine cocktail remorse to come into play, because wine cocktail drinking, like all cocktail drinking, is about having a good time.

To help you out, *Wine Cocktails* is broken into easy-to-use chapters covering the four main groups: red/rosé, white, sparkling, and other (sherry, sake, and the like). Each recipe does have a suggested type of wine (with backup suggestions if I think the wine might be more difficult to get). You'll see, even if you haven't spent much time holding stemware, a lot of familiar faces. While there are a number of particular wines that best match up with specific drinks, certain wines show up multiple times. In the white wine chapter, for example, Riesling is often suggested, as its balance of sugar and acidity, as well as its often delicate undertones, mixes well in multiple situations. In the same way, Cabernet Sauvignon shows up in multiple red wine recipes, due to its rich flavor and bouquet.

The recipes do cover some ground in the wine they use (which is great, because it means you'll find recipes for all occasions). If you're not a wine aficionado, don't let this worry you. Everything called for is readily available. And anyway, experimenting with something you haven't tried, haven't yet enjoyed, or don't remember having is fun. If you've been warned against drinking rosé wine, for instance, you shouldn't shy away from the Rosé Squirt. Rosé for the past few decades has been a maligned wine (perhaps because for a long time it was overly sweet and sort of vile), but it has risen in both quality and stature, and when mixed with maraschino liqueur and club soda, it makes an absolutely fantastic summer refresher. In the same way that better rosé wines are available, we also can get better-quality dessert wines, and other wines from around the world. Sake, wine's Asian cousin, fits into this genre, as more and more types of better-quality sake are now available in the United States. This is good news for us wine cocktailers, because sake mixes up so well in a variety of drinks. Leave any fears at the door, or you'll miss out on drinks that feature some of these lesser-known wine relatives, relatives like sherry (it's not just for sipping when you're visiting Oxford), port, or my Canadian friends' favorite, ice wine (made using frozen grapes—really). The key is not to be afraid or worried if you have a lack of knowledge. There's no snobbery with wine cocktails; they exist solely to give you a chance to try, and serve, new and entertaining drinks.

Listen Up for the Liquor Talk

We can't forget that many of the stunning sippers in this book also use a type of liquor or liqueur (or both), and that these ingredients are just as important as the wine component. When thinking about your base liquors (here I'm talking about gin, vodka, brandy, whiskey/bourbon, and tequila), it's good to follow some of the suggestions I just gave for wine. While I love the super-premium liquors, I love them most in solo style. Don't get me wrong—if you want to use a high-end, expensive vodka in your Maibowle, I won't hold it against you. But neither would I if you chose a middle-range liquor. For example, I always use Maker's Mark bourbon when making a Magic Man—it fits in perfectly with the other ingredients, and doesn't involve taking out a second mortgage.

Beyond the base liquors, many of these wine cocktail recipes call for some type of liqueur. We're extremely lucky today that more and more liqueurs from around the globe are available, and more are being created every day (not to mention that it can be fun making your own). Because of this liqueur globalization, it shouldn't be hard to find the liqueurs used in this book (from Aperol to Strega and everything in between). If you do have a hard time locating them at your local liquor store, then try ordering online (www.internetwines.com has a reliable selection).

Mixers, Garnishes, and Ice Must Make a Speech

We've talked a bit about wine, and chatted about liqueurs and liquors, but there are a couple final ingredient categories that need to be mentioned: mixers, garnishes, and ice. Mixers, for this discussion, include the nonalcoholic items added to a drink during construction (garnishes would be added at the end of construction). I'm talking everything from fresh fruit, fresh fruit juice, and herbs to ginger ale and club soda. There's a handy rule to remember when picking out and putting together your mixers: the "fresh" rule. This means that you want to use freshly squeezed juices whenever possible and also fresh fruit (when shopping watch out for brown spots on the fruit, which you want to avoid; don't be afraid to pick up, smell, and even talk to the fruit before buying), both for juicing and for muddling. But it doesn't stop there. When using mint to make a C&C, make sure your mint isn't bruised, brown, or slimy. And, when using ginger ale, club soda, or other carbonated mixer, don't reopen an old bottle or your drinks won't have enough fizziness. Your bubbly mixer should open with a hearty hiss (and maybe even some explosiveness), not a weak *pfff*. Remember to go fresh, and you'll become the wine cocktail slinger your friends talk about in awed tones.

With that said, there are two very important mixers that slightly (not completely) circumvent the "fresh" rule. The first one is simple syrup (below). Simple syrup is a basic, easy-to-make mixture of sugar and water used in many drinks, enough drinks that I think it's good to always have a bottle of it around. In the fridge, it should stay in good shape for about a month, provided you put it in a bottle that seals nice and tight. But I'll bet once you get acquainted with using it (it's great not only for sparkling cocktails, but also for non-boozy beverages like fresh lemonade), you won't have to worry about it hanging around longer than a month.

Our final crucial mixer is bitters, a mysterious amalgamation of herbs, spices, roots, fruits, and other magical items in liquid form, designed specifically to add extra notes and excitement to drinks. Sadly, bitters were almost forgotten at one point. But over the past few years, bitters have been making a brilliant comeback. There are now a number of different kinds available, including Angostura (which is the best known), Peychaud's, Regan's Orange Bitters, and the Fee Brothers line of flavored bitters. You can find these enchanting flavor enhancers in grocery and gourmet stores, specialty shops, some liquor stores, and online.

After putting all these mixers together with wine and liqueurs and liquors (or some combination thereof), you're ready to serve something up, right? Well, sometimes, but there are many drinks in this book that just

SIMPLE SYRUP
Makes about 4 ½ cups

2½ cups water 3 cups sugar	**1.** Combine the water and sugar in a medium-size saucepan. Bring the mixture to a boil over medium-high heat, stirring occasionally. Lower the heat a bit, keeping the mixture at a low boil for 5 minutes. **2.** Turn off the heat and let the syrup cool completely in the pan. Store in a clean, airtight container in the refrigerator.

don't make the grade without the right garnish. Not only do garnishes add that visual accoutrement that some fashionable drinks require, but they also tend to instill a bit more flavor to the drink's taste. Without actually twisting a lemon twist over your Lord Charles so that the essential oils from the rind are expelled, the drink should really only be called a "Charles" because it's without a crucial part. With garnishes, it's also a requirement that you remember the "fresh" rule. Without that, your garnishes go from glorious to goofy to even inducing growls from your guests. Fresh, blemish-free fruit and herbs are the good garnisher's best friend.

Even though not all garnishes come in the form of citrus fruit (strawberries are a great garnish with sparkling wine drinks, for example, and a mint sprig livens up the Witch in White), it's good to know how to make the three main citrus garnishes, as they do show up on a regular basis. Those three garnishes are twists, wheels, and wedges. We'll chat up twists first, which involve a simple process. First, cut the bottom end of a fruit off in a straight line, taking only enough of the fruit to construct a flat surface. Then, place the flat part of the fruit on your cutting board. Using a garnishing knife or paring knife, cut off ½-inch-wide strips of peel, cutting from top to bottom, working to get as little inner pith as possible while still having a sturdy strip, as these strips are your twists and need to be strong enough to be twisted over your drink (this twisting is accomplished by holding each end of the fruit peel strip and then turning your hands in opposite directions). You should be able to see the oil expelled into the drink when you twist.

Wheels and half-wheels (also called slices) are a breeze to make. Simply slice the ends off your citrus fruit, aiming to get about ⅛ inch off each end. Then slice the fruit into uniform wheels, notching the wheels as needed to balance them on the rim of a glass. Cut a wheel in half and you've got a slice.

Our final citrus garnish, the wedge, is also pretty simple to make. You begin much like wheels: Cut ⅛ inch off each end of your fruit. Then, slice the fruit in half lengthwise. Place each half, cut side down, on a cutting board and make three cuts from top to bottom, with an end result of three equally sized pieces. Cut those pieces in half (or thirds if you have really large fruit) and you've made it to wedge city.

There's one often-overlooked member of our wine cocktail ingredient list: ice. Except in the odd hot drink or room-temperature mix, ice is a key component, so be sure you don't treat it badly. This means that using old ice that's been in the freezer next to some frozen broccoli isn't going to add much to your drink (unless you want a drink that echoes a patch of past-due vegetables). For this book, most drinks call for regular 1-inch ice cubes, so use those if possible. There are some punches in the book, which work best (and look lovely) with a block of ice. If you have to, you can sub in cracked ice (the kind sold at the store in bags) for punches, and for ice cubes in shaken drinks (though it can add a little extra water to the drink, it shouldn't drag you down too much).

Bar Tool Chatter

While there are a number of bar tools that'll come in handy, one particular item should stand alone at the top of the list when you're stocking your bar: the cocktail shaker. Not every drink in this book requires a cocktail shaker, but enough do that you'll be pretty sad without one. When picking out your cocktail shaker, you have two possibilities, the Cobbler shaker or the Boston shaker. The Cobbler shaker has been used by cocktail aficionados almost since cocktails themselves were in existence, and it's really a snap to use. It has a bigger bottom receptacle piece covered by a smaller top lid piece that fits snugly into the bottom piece. The top piece tends to have a strainer built in, as well as a cap that can double as a measuring device. To use a Cobbler shaker is easy-peasy: Add ice and ingredients to the bottom piece, then secure the top (remember to get it in tight), and then shake, shake, shake (whichever shaker you choose, I suggest shaking for at least 10 to 15 seconds). Then remove the cap, strain into glasses, garnish as needed, and serve. When picking out your shaker be sure that you select one that's 18/10 stainless steel; as your shaker's the top dog amongst bar tools, you'll want to get a shiny (and durable) one.

The Boston shaker has a glass bottom cup and a top cup made of metal (which should also be 18/10 stainless steel if you go the Boston route). While the Boston shaker may be a smidge more difficult to use than the Cobbler, it's not too hard by any means (and both styles deliver frothy icy cocktails). To begin, just add your ice and ingredients to the bottom cup and insert the metal top cup into the bottom cup. Then, carefully (there's no need for spillage) give the bottom of the metal cup a little thump with the palm of your hand to create a seal between the two cups. Holding both pieces (one in each hand), shake, shake, shake, then place the shaker metal side down on a flat surface and, again, carefully thump or nudge the metal piece with your palm or hand to break the seal. You'll then need to use a separate strainer to strain the drink into a glass before garnishing and serving.

There are a number of other tools you'll want to invest in, to make your wine-cocktail-making go smoothly. First, even if your shaker does happen to have a measuring device with it, I think securing a jigger for measuring is a smart idea. Get a jigger that's 18/10 stainless steel and sturdy and has a 1-ounce measuring cup on one side and a 1½- or 2-ounce measuring cup on the other side. This should cover all your cocktail-constructing needs.

As there's a lot of macerated fruit in these wine cocktails, you'll want a durable muddler, which is a wooden tool shaped somewhat like a small baseball bat, tapering from a larger to a smaller end. You use it to work over fruit or herbs to help release juice and the essential oils that add so much oomph to drinks. Watch when picking one out (I suggest trying a restaurant supply store) that you don't end up with one covered in cheap varnish—because you don't want your drinks to end up smelling or tasting like cheap varnish. In addition, since we are making wine cocktails, you'll find that a dependable corkscrew is essential. I love my lever-model Screwpull corkscrew, because it's so quick and easy to use, but you should find whatever corkscrew you're comfortable with, and then keep it within arm's reach during all party situations.

Here are some other tools that are helpful on a regular basis: a paring knife and a chef's knife for garnishing and cutting fruit, some nonslip cutting boards, a juicer (either a lever-model juicer, a juice extractor, or a handheld juicer; remember, fresh juice is scrumptious, and a home juicer will soon become like a best friend), a good stainless-steel ice bucket and ice scoop, a stirring spoon specifically for drinks, more measuring devices (which come in handy when making multiple signature party drinks), a clean bar towel, some creative and colorful bottle stoppers and pourers, and an assortment of snazzy coasters, cocktail napkins, swizzle sticks, and serving trays to give your bar a bit of style.

The Gossip about Glassware

As we're combining wine and cocktails, and both genres have specialized glasses, it's only right that we should go over glassware, starting with a single serious point—glass is always better than plastic. Not only does it look better, but it doesn't seep any plastic-y tastes into the drink. I understand that on occasion resorting to plastic becomes a necessity (it's better to have a drink in a plastic glass than no drink), but whenever possible, use glass and instantly become a better host or hostess. Buying glassware is fun, and there are tons of options out there, with price ranges to fit every budget.

To make the drinks in this book, I suggest you start your glassware collecting with red wine glasses, white wine glasses, cocktail glasses, highball glasses, and Champagne flutes. The red wine glasses have a larger bowl (goblet-style is what you want) and can hold more than a white wine glass, which tends to be slimmer. These sizes match up with the drinks made with these wines, too, as the red wine drinks tend to be a bit heartier, while the white wine drinks tend to be more elegant. The classic cocktail or martini glass, with its well-known design, varies in size from around 3 ounces all the way up to 12 ounces. The smaller ones tend to be found today in antique stores, as most classic cocktails were a little smaller (which isn't a bad thing, because they would stay chilled until the last drop), and it can be quite a hoot to track them down. For the somewhat slender-looking highball glass, you'll want a 10- to 12-ounce model, ideal for the refreshing nature of the tall drinks made within. Pretty and thin, Champagne flutes are ideal for keeping your bubbly drinks bubbling and fresh. Finally, though it's not a glass, I suggest you purchase a shimmery punch bowl and some punch glasses for making the recipes scaled up for a crowd. Nothing looks quite as lovely as a crystal punch bowl filled with a delish drink, and you can pick up very reasonably priced punch bowls in kitchenware stores and antique shops (really, there's no good reason not to have one).

The Last Wine Cocktail Word

Now that we've uncorked this wine cocktail conversation about the ins and outs of getting ready to make and then actually making the delectable drinks on the following pages, there's just one last thing I have to go over, the final key ingredient without which these wine cocktails won't work out nearly as well, and that's fun. Making any kind of drink should be a fun experience, one shared with friends, family, or that special someone. And wine is an especially social, communal beverage. So get on the phone, call up some pals, and start shaking and stirring the wine cocktails. And if the list includes any snooty oenophiles who shake their head at the phrase "wine cocktail," just do whatever it takes to get them to take that first sip, and watch their frowns turn into happy grins.

Ravishing REDS and Refreshing ROSÉS

When they walk into a room, you hear the intake of breath. "Who is that?" people are whispering, in awe of the ravishing array of drinks in this chapter, almost all of which include red wine to bring out their finer fashionable points and to bring out the oohs and aahs from those being served these luscious sippers. If things get too hot, though, you can sidle up to a Rosy Navel, a Perseverance, or a Rosé Squirt, which are made with red wine's close cousin and which take the edge off any hot number.

Aloha Punch
Bishop
Bordeaux Cup
Cabernet Crusta
Cactus Berry
Kitty Highball
Queen Charlotte
Lord Charles
Sangria
Perseverance
Rosé Squirt
Santa Barbara
Rosy Navel

Aloha **PUNCH**
Serves 8

By Jack Lord, this should transport you (unless you're already there, in which case you're lucky already) to one of Hawaii's sandy beaches, surrounded by seaside splendor and wholly solvable crimes. Let's skip the actual crimes, and instead have you (reading short mystery stories) surrounded by tropical seaside splendor and people who are fittingly attired. To complete the picture, make your Aloha Punch with Ulupalakua red, an easygoing medium-dry red wine that boasts berry and spicy flavors (try ordering it from www.mauiwine.com). If you can't find it, any mellow red wine that's on the lighter side will work well.

Ice (in block form if possible, or use cracked ice)

One 750-milliliter bottle red wine

8 ounces fresh pineapple juice

4 ounces fresh lime juice

4 ounces fresh orange juice

2 liters chilled ginger ale

1 lime, cut into wedges

1 orange, cut into slices

1. Put the block of ice in a punch bowl. If using cracked ice, fill the bowl just about halfway.

2. Add the red wine and the fruit juices. Using a wooden spoon or a small surfboard, stir briefly.

3. Add the ginger ale and stir again. Drop in the lime wedges and the orange slices and stir once more. Serve in punch cups or goblets, making sure a little fruit finds its way into each cup.

A QUOTE: "Quickly, bring me a beaker of wine, so that I may wet my mind and say something clever."

—Aristophanes, Greek playwright

BISHOP

Serves 4

"Striding out of the dark places to save the innocent and punish the guilty with a serious rap on the head from the crook of his staff, it's . . . the Bishop." Doesn't that sound like a 1950s TV series that should have been? I suggest, if you can pull it off, going for a slightly English agent-of-justice feel and look when sipping the Bishop, because it sounds like there should be a slightly daring, perhaps a shade shadowy, slightly off-color do-gooder sipping this drink. If that seems a bit much, then maybe just serve these up when playing a dangerous game of dominoes (it helps in dominoes to have a little divine aid at times).

4 lemon wheels	**1.** Combine the lemon wheels and simple syrup in a cocktail shaker. Muddle well with a muddler or long staff of some sort.
3 ounces Simple Syrup (page 13)	
Ice cubes	**2.** Fill the cocktail shaker halfway full with ice cubes. Add the rum. Shake well, while keeping an eye out for evildoers.
4 ounces rum	
8 ounces full-bodied red wine (I suggest a Cabernet Sauvignon)	**3.** Add a few ice cubes to each of 4 sturdy red wine glasses or goblets. Strain the mix over the ice.
4 lemon slices for garnish	**4.** Top off each glass with 2 ounces of red wine. Stir briefly, but seriously. Garnish with the lemon slices and serve.

BORDEAUX *Cup*

Serves 6

The "cup" family of drinks once was large and expanded like kudzu, taking on many forms and variations much like that invasive plant. For this iteration I'm going to go back to one of the sources, The Professor, Jerry Thomas, who was one of the original celebrity bartenders and whose 1862 book *Bar-Tender's Guide or How to Mix Drinks* was one of the first drink compendiums. In it, he has a recipe for a chilled Claret Cup, which, when subbing in a Bordeaux for a little more body and making a few modern alterations, will take the edge off a heated afternoon. As he says, "This is a nice summer beverage for evening parties."

1 lemon

One 750-milliliter bottle Bordeaux

3 ounces Simple Syrup (page 13)

½ cup cold water

½ teaspoon ground cinnamon

½ teaspoon ground cloves

½ teaspoon ground allspice

Ice cubes

1. Using a sharp peeler or paring knife, remove the rind from the lemon, working to get only rind and leaving the white pith behind. Chop the lemon rind into 1- to 2-inch pieces.

2. Combine the Bordeaux, simple syrup, water, cinnamon, cloves, and allspice in a large pitcher. Stir well.

3. Add the lemon rind to the pitcher and stir again briefly.

4. Fill 6 goblets halfway full with ice cubes. Pour the mixture into the goblets, making sure each gets a little lemon rind, and serve.

A NOTE: There are many Bordeaux varieties (all being wine produced in the region of the same name), and some prices can run high. As you're mixing it here, I would go for basic "Red Bordeaux" or "Bordeaux Supérieur," which are fruity and a bit oaky and which fall into the middle range of the cost spectrum.

Cabernet CRUSTA

Serves 2

The Crusta family has a very long lineage. But this merger of juices, wine, and liquor is too distinguished in looks, taste, and preparation to let any question of how old it is bring it— or you—down.

Sugar

3 orange slices

1 orange

Ice cubes

3 ounces Cabernet Sauvignon

1 ounce orange curaçao

½ ounce fresh orange juice

2 ounces Simple Syrup (page 13)

4 dashes Angostura bitters

1. Chill 2 basic red wine glasses, either by placing them in the freezer for an hour or more, or by swirling ice around inside them then drying them. Pour a small layer of sugar onto a saucer or plate. Delicately wet the outside of the rim of each wine glass with an orange slice. Then, carefully holding the glass by the stem, rotate the glass through the sugar, so that the sugar coats only the outside of the rim.

2. Using a sharp paring knife or peeler, carefully peel the rind off the orange, in one long spiral strip, avoiding the pith as much as possible. Cut it in half and carefully place a spiral in each wine glass.

3. Fill a cocktail shaker halfway full with ice cubes. Add the Cabernet, curaçao, orange juice, simple syrup, and bitters. Shake vigorously.

4. Add a few ice cubes to each glass, working to ensure the orange rind stays between ice and glass (for nice visuals). Strain the Crusta into the glass. Garnish with the remaining orange slices and serve.

A VARIATION: There are many varieties of Crusta, including variations that use brandy, rum, whiskey, and other liquors. You might try a white wine version, though, using a full-bodied but fruity white wine. Sometimes the Crusta is made with lemon juice and rind rather than orange—a worthy experiment.

CACTUS *Berry*

Serves 2

D on't be afraid: The Cactus Berry (a cousin of the margarita that's taken a trip into a winery) doesn't involve any small piercing thorns that might turn a south-of-the-border soirée into a quick trip to the local first-aid station for cheek stitching. This mix does have a bit of a bite, though, so you'll want to ensure your safety by doing any sort of hat dancing, attempts at tangoing, or cactus scaling earlier in the evening.

Ice cubes

3 ounces Merlot

3 ounces white tequila

1½ ounces Cointreau

1 ounce fresh lime juice

2 lime slices for garnish

1. Fill a cocktail shaker halfway full with ice cubes. Add the Merlot, white tequila, Cointreau, and lime juice. Shake exceedingly well (as if you were shaking cactus thorns from your hands).

2. Strain the mix into 2 cocktail glasses. Garnish with the lime slices and serve.

A QUOTE: "Wine to the poet is a winged steed / Those who drink water gain but little speed."

—Nicaentus, Greek poet

Kitty HIGHBALL
Serves 4

The Kitty uses claret for a tall refreshing drink that I judge ideal for being quaffed by anyone playing croquet or perhaps pondering a game of croquet. While claret refers to red wine from the Bordeaux region of France, you won't actually hear that word used when in France as it's an English term that refers to this usually darker red (though, between us friends, the word comes from the French word *clairet*, which means "pale," as the wine in question used to be a rosé). Whew, that's a bit to remember. Which is why I think sticking to croquet while drinking the Kitty (as opposed to any deep-thought kind of exercising) is a dandy plan.

Ice cubes	**1.** Fill 4 highball glasses three-quarters full with ice cubes. Add 3½ ounces claret to each glass. Top each with ginger ale, until almost to the top of the glass. Stir 6 times.
14 ounces claret (or Bordeaux)	
Chilled ginger ale	**2.** Twist a lemon twist, if desired, over each glass and drop it in. Serve immediately.
4 lemon twists for garnish (optional)	

A NOTE: I enjoy the little burst of lemon here; if you don't, don't worry your pretty little head. I won't come your way with an idea of "tapping the claret."

A SECOND NOTE: "Tapping the claret" is an older English expression for giving a bloody nose. But I'm a cocktail lover, not a fighter.

Queen CHARLOTTE

Serves 2

Good evening, lords and ladies and gentlefolk of the celebrating court. If you would please doff your tiaras and poofy purple hats, tuck back your capes and robes, still your lips for a second from flapping that festive talk, set down the turkey leg, pull on your booties and stand in silence while she enters the grand ballroom under the chandeliers, and then take a deep breath, we can (together, the way it should be) all hail the queen.

Ice cubes	**1.** Fill a cocktail shaker halfway full with ice cubes. Add the vodka, grenadine, and red wine. Shake well.
2 ounces vodka	
1 ounce grenadine	**2.** Fill 2 diamond-, ruby-, or garnet-encrusted goblets three-quarters full with ice cubes. Strain the red wine mixture equally over the ice in each glass. Top with 7UP, until just about $^1/_2$ inch below the rim.
6 ounces full-bodied red wine (see A Note)	
Chilled 7UP or Sprite	

A NOTE: A serious California or French Syrah or Australian Shiraz works well here.

A SECOND NOTE: If you feel this needs a garnish to really become royalty, then I suggest a single simple lemon twist.

Lord CHARLES

Serves 2

Having a royalish celebration where Lord Charleses and Queen Charlottes (page 29) are the signature drinks is bound to be the crown jewel of any party season. Hand out crowns and coronets (even if they're just made of paper and paste), serve some kingly snacks (perhaps those chocolate gold coins?), play a little French horn music (which seems somehow majestic), and who knows, maybe a real lord and lady will show up in a coach. Or maybe you'll turn into a pumpkin at midnight. Either way, it'll be revelry to remember.

Ice cubes

4 ounces Malbec

2 ounces Simple Syrup (page 13)

1 ounce fresh lemon juice

2 ounces dry sherry

Chilled club soda

2 lemon twists for garnish

1. Fill a cocktail shaker halfway full with ice cubes. Add the Malbec, simple syrup, lemon juice, and sherry. Shake well.

2. Fill 2 highball glasses three-quarters full with ice cubes. Strain the Malbec mixture equally over the ice cubes in each glass. Fill each glass with club soda, almost to the rim.

3. Twist a lemon twist over each glass and drop it in. Stir briefly with a scepter or stir stick and serve.

A NOTE: Malbec has characteristics that fall between Cabernet Sauvignon and Merlot, with a deep color and rich flavor with significant tannins. It's one of the premier wines of Argentina, and Malbecs from that country (where it's sometimes called "Malbeck") are delicious.

A QUOTE: "Wine comes in at the mouth / And love comes in at the eye; / That's all we shall know for truth / Before we grow old and die."
—W.B. Yeats, "A Drinking Song"

SANGRIA
Serves 6

A classic wine drink, Sangria, when made with the right balance of wine, fruit, and other alcohols, is an ideal mate for a wide assortment of mid-to-large gatherings, from baseball watching to back-porch jamborees to hat-dancing fiestas. When you whip up the first pitcher (it should always be made by the pitcherful), people might be a bit wary, having experienced their fair share of disastrous restaurant versions. But after the first sip of this passes their lips, they'll realize what a good Sangria really tastes like.

1 orange, cut into wheels

1 lemon, cut into wheels

1 lime, cut into wheels

6 ounces Simple Syrup (page 13)

4 ounces fresh orange juice

2 ounces fresh lime juice

One 750-milliliter bottle medium-bodied dry red wine

6 ounces brandy

Ice cubes

Fresh fruit slices (oranges, limes, lemons, apples) for garnish

1. Place the orange, lemon, and lime wheels and simple syrup in a large glass pitcher. Muddle well with a muddler and a good reach or a wooden spoon.

2. Add the orange juice and lime juice and muddle just a touch more.

3. Add the red wine and brandy and stir well (bring a guest stirrer in if needed). Place the pitcher carefully in the refrigerator for 2 hours or more, but no longer than 36 hours.

4. Add ice until the pitcher is full and stir slightly. Pour into 6 stemmed wine glasses or goblets and garnish with fresh fruit as desired.

A VARIATION: White Sangria adds a nice twist to the formula. To make it, substitute 1 bottle dry white wine (choose one with just a bit of fruit accents, such as a drier Riesling or a French Pinot Gris) for the red, 3 ounces white grape juice for the lime juice, and 1 apple, cut into slices, for the lime wheels.

PERSEVERANCE

Serves 2

Originally a drier, crisp wine made in France and certain other parts of Europe (it's called rosato in Italy), rosé started to gain sweetness in the middle part of the last century, and then in the United States in the 1970s it experienced a surge in both sweetness and popularity due to the sugary blush wines whose coloring it resembles (though the process used to make them is different). But a good wine perseveres, and the drier, European-style rosé has made a comeback. In this cocktail, whose name matches the wine's persistence, the dry, delicate flavor pairs with vodka, maraschino liqueur, and a bit of bitters for a complex and completely satisfying drink.

Ice cubes	**1.** Fill a cocktail shaker halfway full with ice cubes. Add the vodka, rosé, maraschino liqueur, and bitters. Shake well.
1 ounce vodka	
2 ounces dry rosé	**2.** Strain the Perseverance equally into 2 cocktail glasses and serve.
½ ounce maraschino liqueur	
2 dashes Peychaud's bitters	

A NOTE: I think Fat Bastard's rosé works dandy in this drink. Look for it in your local wine shop or online.

ROSÉ *Squirt*

Serves 2

H ey, are you having a flashback to summers when those big grouchy kids were bringing you down, taking your hat, calling you squirt? Don't let those memories tarnish your sunshiny afternoons and evenings. Remember two things and you'll be able to relax in suitable summer fashion. First, those kids were just jealous (and would be even more so if they knew about the beautiful hot-weather bashes you have now), and second, you have the last laugh because you now know that the Squirt is a tall, refreshing, bubbly drink that goes with a backyard barbecue or luscious lawn party, or with sitting with that perfect person as the sun goes down in July.

Ice cubes	**1.** Fill 2 highball glasses three-quarters full with ice cubes. Add 1 ounce maraschino liqueur and 3 ounces rosé to each glass. Stir briefly.
2 ounces maraschino liqueur	
6 ounces dry rosé	**2.** Fill each glass almost to the top with the chilled club soda. Stir again, a bit more than briefly. Drop a cherry on top and serve.
Chilled club soda	
2 maraschino cherries for garnish	

A NOTE: Don't be fooled into thinking that maraschino liqueur is the same as the liquid that comes with maraschino cherries in the jar or as cherry syrup. Instead, it's made from the fruit and pits of marasca cherries, with a dry, rich flavor that has hints of both cherries and almonds.

Santa BARBARA
Serves 2

As the town of Santa Barbara is sometimes called the "American Riviera" due to its Mediterranean-esque climate, it is demanded (by the wine cocktail patrol, I suppose) that you adapt a style that matches. So plan on wearing clothes that are classically fashionable while allowing for serious relaxation as you sit and sip the drink sharing that California town's name, perhaps daydreaming about a real Mediterranean escape from daily doldrums (unless you already are in the Mediterranean, in which case I'm wishing I were you).

Ice cubes	**1.** Fill a cocktail shaker halfway full with ice cubes. Add everything but the twists, but add them with a bit of smooth style. Shake well (but again, keep a little style here).
1 ounce fresh lemon juice	
1 ounce Simple Syrup (page 13)	**2.** Strain the mixture into 2 cocktail glasses. Twist a lemon twist over each glass and let it slide in without a second glance. Serve immediately.
2 ounces triple sec	
3 ounces Italian Chianti	
2 lemon twists for garnish	

A NOTE: Another sturdy Italian red, such as Nero d'Avola, will also work here.

A QUOTE: "At friendly meetings, and when the wine was to his taste, something eminently human beaconed from his eye."
—Robert Louis Stevenson, *The Strange Case of Dr. Jekyll and Mr. Hyde*

ROSY *Navel*

Serves 4

The Rosy Navel's refreshing nature is a dandy companion for those lazy afternoons when the mercury's high on the thermometer and your main goal for the day is relaxing in a swimsuit under the hot sun with a chilly drink. Just be careful, as the last thing you want is to fall asleep in the sun and end up with a sunburned navel.

Ice cubes	**1.** Fill a cocktail shaker halfway full with ice cubes. Add the orange juice, curaçao, and rosé. Shake well.
4 ounces fresh orange juice	
2 ounces orange curaçao	**2.** Fill 4 highball glasses three-quarters full with ice cubes. Strain the mixture equally into the glasses. Top each glass off almost to the top with chilled 7UP. Stir briefly and serve.
8 ounces dry rosé	
Chilled 7UP or Sprite	

A NOTE: Rosé wine is produced all over the world, but be careful what you pick up. Most European varieties are drier, which generally works well whether drinking straight or mixing in cocktails. Stay away from wines called "blush," as they tend to be sweeter, and also please don't make the mistake of thinking that a white Zinfandel is a rosé wine.

Walk into the World of *WHITE WINE*

I t's elegant, refined, and graceful—but still ready to whoop it up at any celebration, from swank soirées to hearty hoe-downs. It's a tall refreshing quaff (like the Moraine Cooler), a strained sustainer (like the C & C), a bowl filled with fun for a whole posse of pals (like the Fremont Fruit Bowl), and a little romance just for two (like the Papa Loves Mama). It's a combination of ingredients with a highlight on the vast choices found in the "whites" aisle of the wine store. It's the wonderful world of white wine cocktails. What are you waiting for? Come on and cross into white wine cocktail country.

Muskrat
Chic Beach
Blue Wave
Maibowle
Loire Lemonade
C & C
Fremont Fruit Bowl
Moraine Cooler
Papa Loves Mama
Witch in White
Whistling Orange
Refroidisseur

MUSKRAT

Serves 2

Can't stop . . . must sing Captain & Tennille hit "Muskrat Love" changed slightly to be about this white wine mixer: "and they muddled and they muddled and they shook, while singin' and jingin' the jingo, floatin' like the pineapple above, it looks like muskrat love." Ah, why resist? After a few Muskrats it's going to sound like a hit no matter the words. This drink was originally made with some variety of Muscatel wine. There are many, many wines that use the Muscat grape, and they run the gamut, though they tend to be sweeter. I think not going overboard on the sweetness is the way to go here, though. With that in mind, I'd suggest a white wine that has just a little sweet in it. If you can get Conundrum white wine from California, it's an ideal choice, with its blend of Sauvignon Blanc, Chardonnay, and Muscat Canelli. Otherwise, use a Chardonnay that has a nice fruit balance and isn't oaky.

½ cup fresh mint leaves	**1.** Combine the mint leaves and pineapple juice in a cocktail shaker or mixing glass. Using a muddler or a wooden spoon, muddle the mint and juice well.
2 ounces pineapple juice	
Ice cubes	**2.** Fill the cocktail shaker halfway full with ice cubes. Add the apricot liqueur. Shake well.
2 ounces apricot liqueur	**3.** Strain the mixture equally into 2 white wine glasses. Top off each with 4 ounces of the white wine. Stir briefly and serve.
8 ounces chilled white wine	

A QUOTE: "Wine is one of the most civilized things in the world and one of the most natural things of the world that has been brought to the greatest perfection, and it offers a greater range for enjoyment and appreciation than, possibly, any other purely sensory thing."

—Ernest Hemingway, *Death in the Afternoon*

Chic BEACH

Serves 2

I believe you should be wearing a bit of high-fashion swimwear around a pool with pals or on the beach beside that certain someone while sipping this tropical tempter. Having said that, if you show up at my pool (an old claw-foot tub in the backyard) wearing cutoffs while carrying the fixings for a Chic Beach, I certainly won't turn you away. And I suggest you cop the same attitude.

Ice cubes

3 ounces white rum

1 ounce orange curaçao

1 ounce fresh lime juice

1 ounce passion fruit syrup

8 ounces chilled white wine (I suggest a fruitier Sauvignon Blanc)

2 lime slices for garnish

1. Fill a cocktail shaker halfway full with ice cubes. Add the rum, curaçao, lime juice, and passion fruit syrup. Shake well, but while looking away distractedly (because the chic are always a bit distracted watching for paparazzi and such).

2. Strain into 2 white wine glasses. Top each with 4 ounces of the chilled white wine. Garnish with the lime slices and serve.

A QUOTE: "Pour out the wine without restraint or stay, / Pour not by cups, but by the bellyful."

—Edmund Spenser, "Epithalamion"

BLUE *Wave*

Serves 2

C*heers* magazine calls itself the "Beverage Magazine for Full Service Restaurants and Bars." It's comforting to know that these places I love have their very own magazine. *Cheers* is packed with information, as you'd expect, but also boasts recipes such as this one; for all I know, the recipe for the Blue Wave was first printed there. So, here's a "cheers" to *Cheers*, by way of thanks for the introduction to this fruity and hip masterpiece of a white wine mélange.

---

4 green apple slices

2 orange slices

2 kiwi slices

Ice cubes

3 ounces Hpnotiq

5 ounces white wine
(I suggest a drier
German Riesling)

2 ounces fresh
orange juice

6 green grapes

4 ounces chilled
ginger ale

1. Combine the green apple slices, orange slices, and kiwi slices in a cocktail shaker or mixing glass. Using a muddler or wooden spoon, muddle well.

2. Fill the shaker halfway full with ice cubes. Add the Hpnotiq, white wine, and orange juice. Shake well (as if you were actually riding a wave).

3. Add 3 grapes to each of 2 cocktail glasses. Strain the almost-Wave into the glasses, over the grapes. Top each with 2 ounces ginger ale and serve.

A NOTE: Freezing the grapes beforehand is a nice touch, as it helps to keep the drink chilled.

MAIBOWLE
Serves 2

Maibowle, which is sometimes called "May wine," is one of those traditional combinations (in this case, I believe Germanic) that every family has a personal spin on, one for which you could (if you were very intrepid about following leads and talking to small-town folks) find many, many variations. I mean, it is "May wine," a phrase that conjures up all manner of spring suggestions. In this version, I like using strawberries. But other versions use peaches, pineapple, or even woodruff or wild baby's breath. The last one sounds like it might have you dancing among the fairy stones, but maybe that's what spring's about. You also may see this made as a punch, but I believe taking the Maibowle to cocktail status displays reverence for the season.

½ cup fresh strawberries, chopped, plus 2 whole strawberries for garnish

1 ounce Simple Syrup (page 13)

Ice cubes

3 ounces vodka

4 ounces Moselle

1. Combine the chopped strawberries and simple syrup in a cocktail shaker. Using a muddler or wooden spoon, muddle well.

2. Fill the cocktail shaker halfway full with ice cubes. Add the vodka and Moselle. Shake well.

3. Make a small cut in the bottom of the whole strawberries. Now, balance each one (using the cut) on the edge of 2 cocktail glasses. Strain the mixture into the glasses and serve immediately.

A NOTE: Moselle, or Mosel, wines are subtle and flowery, originally produced near the river of the same name in Germany, though they are now also made in California.

A QUOTE: "There is not the hundredth part of the wine consumed in this kingdom that there ought to be. Our foggy climate wants help."

—Jane Austen, *Northanger Abbey*

Loire LEMONADE

Serves 4

I f only the kids in my neighborhood would start selling this lemonade from their corner stand, they'd have college tuition covered
in no time. Now, I'm not suggesting that they make the lemonade,
or try to buy the ingredients (that's where parents come in; with tuition
what it is, my guess is the parents would even help with the shaking).
But seriously, picturesque both in natural surrounding and in man-
made architecture (think chateaus you'd want to holiday in for months
on end), the Loire region in France is also home to a host of fine wines
and fine wineries. I think a Sancerre works well here, but experiment
with other crisp, acidic whites, such as Sauvignon Blanc.

Ice cubes

2 ounces fresh
lemon juice

4 ounces Simple
Syrup (page 13)

4 ounces lemon-
flavored vodka

16 ounces chilled
Sancerre

4 lemon twists for
garnish

1. Fill a cocktail shaker halfway full with ice
cubes. Add the lemon juice, simple syrup, and
vodka. Shake well.

2. Put 2 ice cubes in each of 4 white wine
glasses. Strain the lemon mixture equally into
the glasses. Add 4 ounces Sancerre to each glass
and stir gently (no need to be bruising here).

3. Twist a lemon twist over each glass and
drop it in. Serve immediately.

C & C
Serves 2

Everybody drink C & Cs now. Yeah, yeah, yeah. Shaking what the kids call the booty while drinking a C & C and singing C+C Music Factory's biggest hit is advisable, as long as you're on the first one. By the second, you should be a little more careful. You don't want to a) twist an ankle, or b) twist an ankle and spill your drink. I'm all about the right dance moves (though really, I have none) at the right moment, but the dance moves plus holding a C & C? Be careful out there.

½ cup fresh mint leaves

½ cup fresh raspberries

1 ounce Simple Syrup (page 13)

Ice cubes

4 ounces French Chablis

2 ounces Chambord

1. Combine the mint, raspberries, and simple syrup in a cocktail shaker. Using a muddler or spike heels, muddle well.

2. Fill the cocktail shaker halfway full with ice cubes. Add the Chablis and Chambord. Shake well, and put a little shimmy in it too.

3. Strain into 2 cocktail glasses and serve.

A NOTE: Be sure to use French Chablis, which is made from Chardonnay grapes and is dry and delicious, and not one from another country, where the term *chablis* can be used for a wide variety of grape combinations, resulting in generic, overly sweet wines.

A SECOND NOTE: If you don't mind getting a bit messy, forget the straining in step 3 and just pour the whole drink, ice and all, into 2 large goblets. Call it the C & C & C (the last "C" for "cluttered").

Fremont FRUIT BOWL

Serves 10

I wouldn't bet my favorite piece of art on it, but I might wager $5 that this collective cheerer (adapted from *Adventures in Wine Cookery*, published in 1965 by the Wine Advisory Board) hasn't yet been served in Seattle's once-funky Fremont neighborhood (still funky during the summer solstice parade), or many of the other artsy neighborhoods that dot big cities, keeping them fresh with festivals, galleries, bands, and (one hopes) greatly imaginative house parties. If you live in one of these neighborhoods, or want to transform your own staid 'hood, I advocate a bohemian party featuring the Fremont Fruit Bowl.

3 fresh peaches, pitted and cut into wedges

3 fresh apricots, pitted and cut into wedges

3 cups fresh strawberries, stemmed and quartered

Ice (in block form if possible, or use cracked ice)

5 ounces apricot liqueur

5 ounces maraschino liqueur

One 750-milliliter bottle Riesling

One 750-milliliter bottle chilled brut Champagne or sparkling white wine

1. Put the peaches, apricots, and strawberries in a large punch bowl. Using a wooden spoon, stir them together, being just a little brisk, as you want them to be well mixed.

2. Add the block of ice to the bowl or, if using cracked ice, fill the bowl almost halfway.

3. Add the apricot and maraschino liqueurs. Stir well with your wooden spoon.

4. Add the Riesling and Champagne, concurrently (this makes both feel an equal part of the festivities). Stir well, again. Serve in punch cups, white wine glasses, or sculpted goblets.

A NOTE: I suggest an Australian Riesling here, as they tend to be fruity—and the Australians know how to party.

MORAINE *Cooler*

Serves 2

A refresher from way back when, the Moraine Cooler has little to do with the debris piles, also called moraine, that form around glaciers (or formerly glaciated areas). On the contrary: After a few Moraine Coolers, you'll start moving positively unglacially. You'll "put a little quick in it," as the kids say. With that in mind, wear sensible shoes.

2 lemon wheels	**1.** Put the lemon wheels in a cocktail shaker. Using a muddler or piece of glacial ice that resembles a muddler, muddle well.
Ice cubes	
1½ ounces orange curaçao	**2.** Fill the cocktail shaker halfway full with ice cubes. Add the curaçao and wine. Shake well.
6 ounces white wine (I suggest a Riesling)	**3.** Fill 2 highball glasses halfway full with ice cubes. Strain the Moraine equally into each glass. Top with club soda till it approaches, but doesn't reach, the rim. Stir well. Garnish each with a lemon twist and serve.
Chilled club soda	
2 lemon twists for garnish	

A NOTE: My pick here is for the Riesling from Trio Vintners in Walla Walla, Washington. It's my favorite Riesling in the world (at least so far) and works ideally. (Check it out at www.triovintners.com.) If you can't find it near you, try another off-dry, crisp Pacific Northwest Riesling.

A SECOND NOTE: A shout-out here to Mr. or Mrs. A. Gorishek, who owned my copy of Jacques Staub's *Drinks* back in 1942 (or so it says on the inside flap), which is the book where I first saw the Moraine Cooler. Thanks for keeping the book in such dandy condition.

PAPA *Loves* MAMA
Serves 2

This one's for the happy couples in the house, those loving folks celebrating an anniversary, birthday, holiday, Wednesday, or summer's day together, doing a bit of waltzing, a bit of laughing, and a bit of sipping. Adapted from mid-1900s gadabout, writer, and serious imbiber Crosby Gaige's good-time read *Cocktail Guide and Ladies' Companion*, Papa Loves Mama isn't just for the ladies, though; fellas, trust that you'll get all the hugs you need when you serve your favorite missus this mix.

½ cup fresh raspberries

1 ounce Simple Syrup (page 13)

Ice cubes

3 ounces gin

1 ounce kirsch

3 ounces dry Chardonnay

6 frozen raspberries for garnish

1. Combine the raspberries and simple syrup in a cocktail shaker. Using a muddler or sturdy wooden spoon, muddle well while making moony eyes at your sweetheart.

2. Fill the cocktail shaker halfway full with ice cubes. Add the gin, kirsch, and wine. Shake well, while winking at your favorite wonderful person.

3. Add 3 frozen raspberries to each of 2 cocktail glasses. Strain the mixture equally over the raspberries. Serve immediately.

A NOTE: Kirsch, or kirschwasser, is a young cherry brandy that's dry and not sweet.

A QUOTE: "Mama may fill the shaker with Champagne and it won't injure Papa's feelings. Pour till it hurts and thus she will keep the home fires burning."
—Crosby Gaige's *Cocktail Guide and Ladies' Companion*

WITCH *in White*
Serves 4

S creamin' Jay Hawkins, it's reported in some obscure music magazines, was sipping a Witch in White when he recorded "I Put a Spell on You" in 1957. As he also showed his internationalism in songs such as "I Love Paris," it doesn't surprise me one iota that the blues shock master would favor a sipper that uses the Italian liqueur Strega. Its name means "witch," and it is so called because, as the legend goes, the picturesque town in which it's made (Benevento, Italy) used to be a hangout for witches, who would dance around the maple tree during witch festivals and whatnots.

6 ounces Strega	**1.** Put 1½ ounces Strega and ½ ounce orange juice in each of 4 white wine glasses. Stir just a touch (with a tiny witch's broom if available).
2 ounces fresh orange juice	
Chilled Italian Pinot Grigio	**2.** Fill each glass almost to the rim with the Pinot Grigio. Stir again briefly. Garnish with the mint sprigs and serve.
4 fresh mint sprigs	

A NOTE: As there isn't any ice involved here, be doubly sure your Pinot Grigio is well chilled.

A SECOND NOTE: Just as a warning, after party guests consume three of these (three being the magic number), they probably will start singing the lines, "I put a spell on you, because you're mine." Go with it.

Whistling ORANGE
Serves 4

A charming (some might even say divine) proxy for the better-known mimosa at a Saturday or Sunday breakfast or lunch affair, the Whistling Orange seems a bit urbane, a bit sophisticated, perhaps the David Niven of drinks. Of course, Mr. Niven is also supposed to have said, "I've been lucky enough to win an Oscar, write a bestseller—my other dream would be to have a painting in the Louvre. The only way that's going to happen is if I paint a dirty one on the wall of the gentlemen's lavatory." The Whistling Orange also has this playful side to balance the polish, as after your guests are introduced to the drink they'll want to engage in whistling contests.

8 ounces chilled fresh orange juice 8 dashes orange bitters 24 ounces chilled white wine (I suggest a Sauvignon Blanc or a drier Chardonnay)	1. Put 2 ounces orange juice and 2 dashes orange bitters in each of 4 white wine glasses. Stir slightly. 2. Top off each glass with 6 ounces of the white wine. Stir again and serve.

A NOTE: If this isn't quite to your desired level of chilliness, feel free to add an ice cube or two. It won't diminish the drink's classiness.

REFROIDISSEUR

Serves 2

The Refroidisseur claims its title (and one of its main ingredients) from the lovely and loving French. Following the theme, I suggest serving it up to a paramour on a summer day when you're in a continentally flirtatious kind of mood. Just start by saying in French, "Laisse-moi te refroidir avec cette boisson fraîche, bébé?" The accent alone will turn things your way.

6 lemon slices

10 to 12 fresh mint leaves

1 ounce Simple Syrup (page 13)

Ice cubes

8 ounces white wine (see A Note)

Chilled Perrier or other sparkling water

1. Put 2 of the lemon slices, 5 or 6 of the mint leaves, and ½ ounce of the simple syrup in each of 2 highball glasses. Carefully muddle well with a muddler.

2. Fill the glasses three-quarters full with ice cubes. Add 4 ounces of the wine and stir briefly.

3. Top off each glass (almost to the rim) with the Perrier. Stir again. Garnish each with a remaining lemon slice and serve.

A NOTE: I suggest a dry Vouvray for this, but feel free to sub in a Chenin Blanc.

A TRANSLATION: Just so you don't think I'm steering you wrong, the translation is simply, "Can I cool you down with this cool drink, baby?"

A QUOTE: "A man cannot make him laugh—but that's no marvel; he drinks no wine."

—William Shakespeare, *Henry IV, Part II*

Bounteous BUBBLY

I'm calling you out, you the lover of Champagnes, Proseccos, and sparkling wines of all stripes, including reds and rosés. Don't be shy, because loving the bubbly is a beautiful thing. But to really unveil your bubbly bona fides, dive amongst the cocktails and highballs in this chapter, which rely on a popping bubble base to bring their taste sensations to the drinking public. From riding the Blue Train to getting up close and personal with the VPM (or Vanilla-Pear Mimosa), these effervescent wonders make every evening an event and turn bleary mornings and afternoons into fizzy paradises.

Blue Train
Champagne Punch
Champagne Bowler
Frisco Cocktail
French 75
Venetian Spritz
Kir Royale
Lamb's Wool
Magic Man
Vanilla-Pear Mimosa
Valencia
Monks Converge

Blue TRAIN
Serves 2

Whether your idea of relaxing revolves around spinning the hard bop of John Coltrane's *Blue Train* album or reclining on one of the various so-called blue trains (through Eastern Europe, South Africa, or Japan), this bubbly blue mix boasts a base of brandy and pineapple juice that helps ensure that the proper mood is reached, as the drink travels well through both musical time and space.

Ice cubes

3 ounces brandy

2 ounces fresh pineapple juice

Chilled Cap Classique or other sparkling wine (see A Note)

2 pineapple chunks for garnish (optional)

1. Fill a cocktail shaker halfway full with ice cubes. Add the brandy and pineapple juice. Shake well, either in a jazz beat or with a train's rhythmic motion.

2. Strain the mixture equally into 2 flute glasses. Top with the chilled wine. Garnish with a pineapple chunk, skewered on a toothpick, if desired. Travel safely.

A NOTE: Cap Classique is a South African sparkling wine (which I thought would go nicely here, as one of the "blue train" routes goes through South Africa; the taste matches up well too, especially if you use a brut version). Another brut sparkler would also work.

A QUOTE: "I used to like mine with Champagne. The Champagne as cold as Valley Forge and about a third of a glass of brandy beneath it."
—Raymond Chandler, *The Big Sleep*

CHAMPAGNE *Punch*

Serves 10

This Champagne Punch recipe has been handed down through the years in a tightly wound papyrus scroll, with numerous ancient runes traced along the sides, as well as a smattering of mystic graffiti, arcane symbols, and silly faces. They are put there as a curse that says you must serve this in a twinkling punch bowl, and you must be wearing traditional English dinner attire. Otherwise, maybe the sky won't fall, but your Champagne may lose its bubbles. Those old curses are awfully dangerous.

Ice (in block form if possible, or use large chunks)

6 ounces fresh orange juice

2 ounces fresh lime juice

2 ounces fresh lemon juice

4 ounces Simple Syrup (page 13)

6 ounces light rum

6 ounces dark rum

One 750-milliliter bottle brut Champagne, chilled

Orange, lime, and lemon slices for garnish

1. Put the block of ice in a large punch bowl. If using ice chunks, fill the bowl just under halfway.

2. Add the juices and simple syrup. With a large spoon or ladle, stir 10 times (whichever direction you choose—the curse doesn't get specific on stirring).

3. Add the rums. With the same large spoon or ladle, stir 10 more times.

4. Add the Champagne and stir very gently. Add lots of orange, lime, and lemon slices.

5. Ladle into punch glasses, white wine glasses, or historic goblets, working to get a little fruit in each receptacle. Serve immediately.

A VARIATION: There are many great Champagne Punch recipes. Feel free to experiment a little, perhaps subbing in Cointreau or Citrónge for the dark or light rum. Another idea is to sub in fresh pineapple juice for the orange juice. You see how it can work; keep the proportions intact and keep the Champagne as part of it all and everyone will be happy.

CHAMPAGNE *Bowler*

Serves 2

I t should go without saying, but nonetheless, say it I will: You must wear a bowler hat when drinking a Champagne Bowler. Or, at the very least, watch a Chaplin movie or read a little Lucius Beebe (famous bon vivant and bowler-wearer). I first read of this drink in the charmingly wooden-covered 1941 book *Here's How: Mixed Drinks* by W.C. Whitfield, where they "note accent on American products." With this in mind, I suggest using a Domaine Ste. Michelle brut for the sparkler here and a California Chardonnay for the white wine.

6 fresh strawberries	**1.** Combine the strawberries and simple syrup in a cocktail shaker. Using a muddler or sturdy wooden spoon, muddle well.
2 ounces Simple Syrup (page 13)	
Ice cubes	**2.** Fill the cocktail shaker halfway full with ice cubes. Add the Cognac and white wine. Shake well (but don't lose your hat).
1 ounce Cognac	
2 ounces white wine	**3.** Pour everything from the shaker into 2 goblets or large red wine glasses. Top with the sparkling wine. Stir gently and serve.
8 ounces chilled sparkling wine	

FRISCO *Cocktail*

Serves 4

I sure hope someone in the City by the Bay still calls San Francisco "Frisco." Isn't it western-y? And, as Frisco is on the west coast, I hope there are still a few folks partaking of Frisco Cocktails while donning ten-gallon hats, or dusty cowboy boots with spurs, or at least leather chaps. I mean, leave the horses at home (nobody needs to be drinking while riding a horse), but at least for me, and for Frisco, hum a little of the theme from *The Magnificent Seven* and knock back a herd of these brisk favorites.

Ice cubes

6 ounces apricot brandy

4 ounces fresh lemon juice

2 ounces grenadine

Chilled brut Champagne or sparkling wine

4 lemon twists for garnish

1. Fill a large cocktail shaker halfway full with ice cubes. Add the apricot brandy, lemon juice, and grenadine. Shake well.

2. Strain the mixture equally into 4 flute glasses. Top each with chilled Champagne. Garnish with a lemon twist and serve.

A NOTE: To keep the dust off your duds (and glass), I say go with a dry bubbly here, something brut to go with the drink's macho attitude.

A QUOTE: "A statue could not look more imperturbable, and he turns his head but very slightly, with supreme indifference, when peals of laughter, more joyous than common, are wafted through the open windows of the mess-room, where some of our friends have fairly embarked on that tide of good-humour and hilarity which sets in with the second glass of Champagne."

—G.J. Whyte-Melville, *M or N: Similia Similibus Curantur*

FRENCH 75

Serves 2

T his chic beauty of a drink has made a lovely comeback recently. And I, for one (and you, I hope, for two) couldn't be happier, because the French 75 is like a spring day in its fresh balance of sweet and tart. After one or two sipped on the veranda, it's possible to actually reach a spring state of being, as opposed to just being in spring. Have a few—you'll see what I mean.

Ice cubes

2 ounces gin

1 ounce fresh lemon juice

1 ounce Simple Syrup (page 13)

Chilled brut Champagne

2 lemon slices for garnish

2 orange slices for garnish (optional)

2 maraschino cherries for garnish (optional)

1. Put I or 2 ice cubes in each of 2 flute glasses. Add I ounce gin, $^1/_2$ ounce lemon juice, and $^1/_2$ ounce simple syrup to each glass, with an ease that shows you know what spring's about.

2. Top off each flute with Champagne and a lemon slice. If you need more nourishment, also add an orange slice and a cherry. Feel free to connect the garnishes with a toothpick.

A NOTE: If your Champagne is extra chilly, feel free to skip the ice cubes. If it's a very, very toasty spring day, feel free to make this over ice in a highball glass. Even spring needs to be temperate.

A VARIATION: Substitute brandy for the gin and you'll have a French 76. Put in Cognac instead of gin, and you'll have what many think was a French 75 to begin with. David A. Embury (*The Fine Art of Mixing Drinks*, Doubleday, 1956) says that, "Gin is sometimes used instead of cognac in this drink, but then, of course, it no longer should be called French."

VENETIAN *Spritz*
Serves 2

When Italian poet Cesare Pavese wrote, "Sei la luce e il mattino," he wasn't talking about the lovely combination of Prosecco with one of the many various and wondrous Italian liqueurs. But doesn't "you are light and morning" seem to encompass this delicate and light and refreshing blending, a blending that seems to have so many different ways of delighting, much like the sun coming up on a day spent in the center of Italy? I would certainly say so. And I think you'll agree after you taste this classic Italian aperitivo.

3 or 4 ice cubes	**1.** Put 1 or 2 ice cubes in each of 2 flute glasses. Add 1 ½ ounces Aperol to each glass.
3 ounces Aperol	**2.** Fill each glass almost to the rim with the Prosecco and stir gently. Garnish with an orange twist and olive.
About 6 ounces chilled Prosecco	
2 orange twists for garnish	
2 green olives for garnish (not the pimiento-stuffed kind)	

A VARIATION: There are as many variations to this *bella* theme as there are Italian liqueurs and garnishes. For example, my wife suggests a lemon twist, and many like to add a few ounces of sparkling water before the Prosecco. The latter is anathema to me, the former I think a good idea. Instead of Aperol, try Campari, Cynar, the artichoke liqueur (use a lemon twist for sure here), or Strega (my favorite Italian liqueur) without any garnish. Or, to reach heights to sing about, try limoncello, the sun god of Italian liqueurs, with a lemon twist only.

A NOTE: Moscato d'Asti or Asti Spumante both work well here, too. Both are made in the Piedmont region of Italy, near the town of Asti, and are slightly sweet.

KIR *Royale*
Serves 2

Coronations are made for Kir Royales, as are various balls where the gowns cost as much as small cars. In addition, so are the after-parties of dinners of state (since the Kir Royale and Kir were named after Canon Felix Kir, mayor of Dijon, France, from 1945 to 1965), where toasts are made before and after treaties are signed with a pen made from actual peacock feather. Finally, and more practically for us, serve these on any night where either a tiara is worn by one party guest or where *Kind Hearts and Coronets*, *The Lion in Winter*, or any other movie that has a castle or large country home in it is watched.

2 ounces framboise Chilled brut Champagne 2 lemon twists for garnish	Put 1 ounce of framboise in each of 2 flute glasses. Fill the flutes with Champagne. Garnish each glass with a lemon twist and, if you want, a tiny exquisite ball gown.

A NOTE: Framboise is a raspberry-flavored brandy. If you can't manage a bottle, then try Chambord, a black raspberry–flavored liqueur, or crème de cassis, a black currant–flavored liqueur often used in the Kir Royale.

A VARIATION: If you use a dry white wine instead of Champagne, you're drinking a Kir.

A QUOTE: "Champagne for my real friends, real pain for my sham friends."
—Tom Waits

LAMB'S *Wool*
Serves 2

This is the honest truth: When I was approximately 12 years old, I owned 12 sheep of my very own. To my dismay today, I didn't have one of those fancy sheepherder trench coats, but I did have a few pairs of boots, and I tried to have a series of neat sheep names, starting with Bilbo, going through Laverne and Shirley, and descending into things like Flopsy when my imagination petered out. Nowadays, when I want to reminisce about those early agrarian days to my city pals, I always serve up a round of Lamb's Wools. I figure they have to stay and listen to my "back-in-the-day" stories if I've just served them a semi-sparkling mixture.

Ice cubes	**1.** Fill a cocktail shaker halfway full with ice cubes. Add the gin, vermouth, and triple sec. Shake well.
3 ounces gin	
1 ounce dry vermouth	**2.** Strain the mixture equally into 2 flute glasses. Fill each glass almost to the rim with Lambrusco. Garnish each with an orange slice and serve.
1 ounce triple sec	
Chilled Italian Lambrusco	
2 orange slices for garnish	

A NOTE: True Italian Lambrusco is nothing like the American-made sweet stuff. Look for something imported and labeled *frizzante* (slightly effervescent). You also want the dry kind rather than the semisweet kind. There are (be careful—you don't want to be fleeced) a number of bottles (and—gasp!—boxes) you'll see labeled "Lambrusco," but be sure you get the real thing.

Magic MAN
Serves 2

This drink wasn't named after Harry Houdini. But when I consume these, I contemplate him, because of how this collection of disparate elements comes together to escape the mundane and become a strong but scrumptious merger that'll dazzle guests like Harry H. dazzled crowds. Make this with a good sparkling rosé; much like Houdini was overlooked at times by certain classes, rosé sparklers are sometimes overlooked as being unworthy. In fact, a good sparkling rosé (usually made by adding a bit more Pinot Noir or instilling a bit more contact with Pinot Noir skins) is a complex and elegant wine.

---

4 sprigs fresh rosemary

1 ounce Simple Syrup (page 13)

Ice cubes

1 ounce orange curaçao

1 ounce Benedictine

4 ounces bourbon

Chilled sparkling rosé

1. Combine 2 sprigs rosemary and simple syrup in a cocktail shaker. Using a muddler, wooden spoon, or magic wand, muddle well.

2. Fill the cocktail shaker halfway full with ice cubes. Add the orange curaçao, Benedictine, and bourbon. Shake well.

3. Strain the Magic equally into 2 flute glasses. Top off each flute with the chilled sparkling rosé and garnish with 1 of the remaining rosemary sprigs. Serve immediately.

A NOTE: Seek out a nice mid-range rosé from France or the Pacific Northwest. Don't be fooled by the overly sweet mixtures you might find in the discount aisle.

Vanilla-Pear MIMOSA
Serves 2

This flavorful bubbly melody only has one fault, I believe. Here's a drink that uses the Italian sparkling wine Prosecco, vanilla vodka, and pear nectar, a unique and sumptuous blend of worldly ingredients, an amalgamation of flavors that are at home with a chocolate croissant in the A.M. or with a little chocolate and cheese later in the P.M., a drink deserving of abundant kind words, and yet it lives with a bland name borrowed from a distant cousin. The next time you're serving this to a group of imaginative revelers (which I'm sure all your friends are), spend some time coming up with a better name for this drink. Send it to me care of The Harvard Common Press, and we'll set this fault right.

Ice cubes

3 ounces vanilla-flavored vodka

1½ ounces pear nectar

Chilled Prosecco

1. Fill a cocktail shaker halfway full with ice cubes. Add the vodka and pear nectar. Shake well (while thinking, "What name approximates the essence of these things I'm combining?").

2. Strain the to-be-renamed mixture equally into 2 flute glasses. Top off each glass with Prosecco. Let your imagination loose.

A NOTE: Pear nectar can be found in bottles in many grocery stores and gourmet shops.

A QUOTE: "The feeling of friendship is like that of being comfortably filled with roast beef; love, like being enlivened with champagne."
—Samuel Johnson, as quoted in *The Life of Samuel Johnson* by James Boswell

VALENCIA

Serves 2

In certain tomes of bar lore and recipes from the early-to-middle part of last century, you always find a Valencia Cocktail #1, followed directly by the Valencia Cocktail #2. The similarities? Apricot brandy, orange juice, and orange bitters. The difference? Champagne. Then, in the middle-to-just-past-middle of the century, you stop seeing option #2. This lack of bubbly is a crying shame. While the straight cocktail version of the Valencia is not bad at all, adding the Champagne takes this into another, more elegant, dimension. You can serve it dressed up, or dressed down, and your guests will be coo-cooing in no time. And you'll be part of the movement that ensures the Valencia made with Champagne is not forgotten.

Ice cubes

4 ounces apricot brandy

2 ounces fresh orange juice

6 dashes orange bitters

Chilled extra dry Champagne

2 orange twists for garnish (optional)

1. Fill a cocktail shaker halfway full with ice cubes. Add the brandy, orange juice, and orange bitters. Stir well with a spoon or attractive stir stick.

2. Strain the mixture equally into 2 flute glasses. Top off each glass with the Champagne and stir once more.

3. Garnish each flute with an orange twist if you'd like. But if not, don't fret the night away.

A NOTE: I think a Champagne labeled extra dry, which will be just a slight smattering sweeter than brut varieties, works wonders here.

A SECOND NOTE: I suggest Regan's Orange Bitters No. 6. It'll cure what ails you.

MONKS *Converge*

Serves 4

Words of wisdom, friends: Never get into a dance contest with a monk. They may walk softly, but with the host of amazing liqueurs that started being made, or are still being made, by monks (not to mention all that scrumptious Belgian beer), I think that when the more casual visitors have walked out of those big wooden doors, many monasteries start to boogie. Also, monks have that great body control (as demonstrated by the martial Shaolin monks), and that tends to translate into serious moves once the dance floor's unveiled. So when the monks converge, it's a serious shindig. One we'll never see, naturally, but I'll bet if you and some close friends bust out full-length robes and this drink, you can approximate it.

Ice cubes	**1.** Fill a cocktail shaker halfway full with ice cubes. Add the gin and Benedictine. Shake well.
4 ounces gin	
3 ounces Benedictine	**2.** Strain the mixture equally into 4 flute glasses (but strain without speaking). Top off each glass with the Champagne. Twist a lemon twist over each glass, drop it in, and serve.
Chilled brut Champagne	
4 lemon twists for garnish	

After-Dinner and Exotic TREATS

A dmit it—you're a bit compulsive (hey, I'm with you). You watch every episode of your favorite TV shows in order (and of course own them), have a spice cabinet that starts with Abraham's Balm and goes to Zwiebel, and avoid meals that don't arrive in shifts. And yet, you're a little unsure about what to serve when the meal's over. Well, my multicourse friend, this is the chapter you've been waiting for, a chapter of drinks made with Vin Santo, sherry, ice wine, sake, and more. Your meals can finally be complete, as the following drinkables are designed to be served after the dinner is done.

Italian Adonis
Bamboo Cocktail
The I-M
Frozen Surfside
Lady Macbeth
Meinbriar Cocktail
Gong
Port Sangaree
Sauternes Mélange
Quarter Deck
Tuxedo
The Sake'd Saint
Sherry Eggnog

Italian ADONIS

Serves 2

I
s it just me, or is there a rather tall, perfectly proportioned man named David in the corner? He's looking off into the distance, out the window, and seems pretty darn confident. I suggest serving him a couple of these and see if that wondrous posing dips a little bit. Or try serving up a couple of these to that smaller intense guy named Michelangelo in the other corner—he could definitely use a drink. As this combination might cause anyone to burst with artistic inspiration, it's right up his Florentine alley.

Ice cubes	**1.** Fill a cocktail shaker halfway full with ice cubes. Add the Vin Santo, sweet vermouth (sometimes called Italian vermouth—see how everything comes together so exactly?), and orange bitters. Shake well.
3 ounces Vin Santo	
3 ounces sweet vermouth	
2 dashes orange bitters	**2.** Strain equally into 2 cocktail glasses and serve. If you feel this needs a garnish, balance a tiny sculptor's trowel on the edge of each glass.

A NOTE: Vin Santo is an Italian dessert wine made from semidried grapes, often served after dinner with biscotti for dunking. If you like, substitute an amontillado sherry in this drink, but then it's just an Adonis. That's okay, but it doesn't quite reach the heights of our Italian hunk.

BAMBOO *Cocktail*

Serves 2

B amboo is legendary for its flexibility: It can be soft and edible, or incredibly hard and used for everything from floors to dishware. This plentiful plant is a symbol of longevity in China and of friendship in India, and is a sacred barrier against evil in Japan. Why, you ask, am I providing this short but informative treatise? Think about it: flexibility, longevity, friendliness, and a barrier against evil; bamboo may be the ideal totem for a host or hostess. I suggest you have a Bamboo Cocktail before and for your next soirée to help you commune with the bamboo spirit and therefore rise to a higher entertaining plane.

Ice cubes	**1.** Fill a cocktail shaker halfway full with ice cubes. Add the sake, dry vermouth, and orange bitters. Shake well, but thoughtfully.
4 ounces extra dry sake	
2 ounces dry vermouth	**2.** Strain equally into 2 cocktail glasses. Serve while remembering the symbol of your reign as ideal party thrower.
4 dashes orange bitters	

A NOTE: There are five main types of sake: Junmai, Honjozo, Ginjo, Daiginjo, and Namazake (which is different from the four other types in that it's unpasteurized and brings together all of the others, giving it a less definable flavor). But there are many flavor shades within the types, and they do sometimes cross borders and can be combined. Picking a particular one in the United States can be difficult, as often bottles won't have the specific type listed. For this drink, I would suggest a Junmai if you can find one (or a sake that is brewed with a high percentage of Junmai, such as Harushika, which is dry and citrusy and refreshing). If you can't find a Junmai, then aim for a solid mid-range sake that says it is "extra dry" and you'll be set.

The I-M
Serves 2

Type type type. Ring ring ring. Click click click. Jabber jabber jabber. Take your fingers away from the keyboard, phone, and any other electronic tethers for a sec, please. I have an important announcement. Your friends, families, and paramours miss having you within physical, as opposed to virtual, reach. Here's a thought. Invite one or two of those folks over tonight, and serve up a few I-Ms (as opposed to sending them) alongside some real conversation. You'll be astounded by how much fun it is.

8 green grapes	**1.** Place 6 of the grapes in a cocktail shaker. Using a muddler or long wooden spoon, muddle them well.
Ice cubes	
4 ounces vodka	**2.** Fill the cocktail shaker halfway full with ice cubes. Add the vodka, ice wine, and dry vermouth. Shake well (while throwing the cell phone, Blackberry, and pager out the window).
2 ounces ice wine	
½ ounce dry vermouth	**3.** Add 1 remaining grape to each of 2 cocktail glasses. Strain the I-M mixture equally over the grapes. Serve with a hug.

Frozen SURFSIDE
Serves 2

Recently rising to fresh heights of chilly popularity, ice wine (or Eiswein) is a dessert wine variety that is made from grapes that have frozen on the vine. When this occurs, the water in the grapes becomes frozen, while the sweet sugars and other grape-y parts stay unfrozen (not to get all chemical, but it's due to differing freezing points). This frostiness goes down (as the ice-wine-loving kids say) before any fermentation. The end product is a nectar that any arctic frost gods would love, as well as any normal old person who doesn't mind a touch of engaging sweetness with their after-dinner wines. In the Frozen Surfside, the ice wine's post-dinner charms mingle agreeably with dry vermouth's herbs and Pernod's anise qualities in a manner that'll bring everyone in from the cold.

Ice cubes

4 ounces ice wine

1 ounce Pernod

1 ounce dry vermouth

2 dashes Angostura bitters

2 lemon twists for garnish

1. Fill a cocktail shaker halfway full with ice cubes. Add the ice wine, Pernod, dry vermouth, and bitters (in that order, to prevent any coolness between ingredients). Shake well.

2. Strain the mixture equally into 2 cocktail glasses. Twist a lemon twist over each glass and let it slip in like the last day of fall before the first freeze. Serve immediately.

A NOTE: Ice wine is now made in many countries around the world, but the most famous are those made in Germany and Canada. The latter country is now the largest producer of ice wines in the world. I particularly like those made near Kelowna, British Columbia.

Lady MACBETH

Serves 4

A fortified wine, specifically from the Douro Valley in northern Portugal, port is usually served solo to calm things down after a large dinner or very bloody play. Today there are many port-style wines (made in many places, including Australia, South Africa, Canada, and the United States), but to really be called port, the product must come from Portugal. While port's dandy alone, I think its rich flavors shine too when mixed with other ingredients. Here ruby port and sparkling wine meet to make a bubbly brilliance (ruby port is the type made most often, and has a lovely claret color and flavor).

8 ounces ruby port	Put 2 ounces port in each of 4 champagne flutes. Top off each glass with sparkling wine. Twist a lemon twist over each drink, drop it in, and serve.
Chilled sparkling wine	
4 lemon twists for garnish	

A NOTE: The other readily available type of port is called "tawny," and it has a nuttier flavor than the ruby. I feel the ruby works best here, but if you only have tawny and want to experiment and I'm one of the guests, I sure won't turn you down.

A SECOND NOTE: I like a drier sparkling wine here (of the brut variety), because it mingles well with the ruby port.

MEINBRIAR *Cocktail*
Serves 2

A curious amalgamation (curiouser and curiouser, Alice might say) of mint, bitters, vermouth, and Marsala (a strong fortified wine made outside of the town of the same name in Sicily, used often in southern Italian cooking and served often with cheese before a meal), the Meinbriar sports a Germanic-sounding moniker but is an Italian affair. The curiouser part comes out because it's a modification of the classic Greenbriar (which is the same drink, made with sherry). I like this variant, and also never believed that curiosity killed the cat (as long as it didn't jump down a rabbit hole with no ending). Instead, it was a lack of Meinbriars that stopped our little feline friend. Don't let this happen to you.

14 to 16 leaves fresh mint	**1.** Combine the mint leaves and bitters in a cocktail shaker. Using a muddler or long wooden spoon, muddle them well.
4 dashes peach bitters	**2.** Fill the cocktail shaker halfway full with ice cubes and lightly muddle the ice and mint and bitters. Add the vermouth and Marsala. Shake exceedingly well.
Ice cubes	
3 ounces sweet vermouth	**3.** Strain the Meinbriar equally into 2 cocktail glasses. Serve with a toothy smile (if nothing else).
4 ounces Marsala	

A NOTE: Can't find the peach bitters? First, try Fee Brothers (www.fee brothers.com). Then, try subbing in a different bitters. But call it an Almost Meinbriar Cocktail.

A VARIATION: Instead of straining into a cocktail glass, strain into a highball glass filled halfway with ice cubes. Then top it off with chilled club soda. Stir well and serve. Call it a Meinbriar Cooler.

A SECOND VARIATION: Not afraid of a little mint in your teeth? Instead of straining, pour the whole mess (mint, ice, and all) into a rocks or old-fashioned glass. Call it a Meinbriar Messy.

GONG

Serves 2

S erve your pals Gongs by the bucketful (well, by the highball-glass-full at least), whether on stage or off, but don't gong them with an actual mallet and musical instrument unless they refuse to show up at your *Gong Show* party dressed as the Unknown Comic, Gene Gene the Dancing Machine, Old Drool, J.P. Morgan, a break-dancing robot, the Popsicle twins, or other favorite (using that term incredibly loosely) from the rousing Chuck Barris years of the afore-mentioned game show. If you have friends who can't get into this clas-sic talent show (without which, would we even have *American Idol*? I sure doubt it), then gong them before even handing them a Gong, because they sure don't deserve this drink.

Ice cubes	**1.** Fill a cocktail shaker halfway full with ice cubes. Add the sake and pomegranate liqueur. Shake well (as if you feared being gonged).
5 ounces sake	
3 ounces pomegranate liqueur	**2.** Fill 2 highball or comparable glasses with ice cubes. Strain the sake–pomegranate mixture equally into the glasses (carefully, again as if you feared gonging).
Chilled ginger ale	
2 orange slices for garnish	**3.** Top off each glass with ginger ale, filling the glass almost to the top. Stir briefly with a thin mallet or long spoon. Garnish each with an orange slice and serve.

A QUOTE: "It is the man who drinks the first bottle of sake, then the second bottle drinks the first, and finally it is the sake that drinks the man."

—Japanese proverb

Port SANGAREE

Serves 4

O h, the Sangaree. Who can tell what you might exactly be? Made differently from sea to sea. Sometimes with port, sometimes with sherry. Not even the ghost of old Jerry (Thomas, that is, the most famous bartender from the mid-1800s). Really, the Sangaree is one of those standards that has fallen a bit out of favor, possibly because everyone had their own spin on how it should be made. I enjoy the port version, but sherry works, and so does Burgundy, and even brandy. There are even versions that use ale or porter and drop the club soda. Just don't, I repeat, don't forget the nutmeg. No one's ever done that, and I sure don't want you to be the first.

Ice cubes	**1.** Fill 4 highball glasses almost to the top with ice cubes. Add ½ ounce simple syrup, then 2 ounces port to each glass.
2 ounces Simple Syrup (page 13)	
8 ounces port (try ruby or tawny— different flavors, good results)	**2.** Fill each glass with club soda. Stir briefly, top each with ¼ teaspoon nutmeg, and serve.
Chilled club soda	
1 teaspoon freshly grated nutmeg	

A QUOTE: "There was a certain richness in his complexion, which I had been long accustomed, under Peggotty's tuition, to connect with port wine."
—Charles Dickens, *David Copperfield*

SAUTERNES *Mélange*

Serves 2

T he "mélange" in this combo's title gives it both a bit of a snooty sound and a bit of an "awkward-grouping-that-may-not-be-for-all" connotation. Both of the above are, and I say this with a disdainful tone, utterly wrong. Using mint, lime, and simple syrup, the Sauternes Mélange is a relative of the mojito and daiquiri, both drinks of the people if ever there were. And those three ingredients go smoothly with the fourth, Sauternes, a French dessert wine renowned for its strength of purpose as well as its smooth sweetness.

10 to 12 leaves fresh mint, plus 2 sprigs for garnish

6 lime wedges

Ice cubes

2 ounces Simple Syrup (page 13)

4 ounces Sauternes

Chilled club soda

1. Combine the mint leaves and 4 of the lime wedges in a cocktail shaker. Using a muddler or wooden spoon, muddle well.

2. Fill the cocktail shaker halfway full with ice cubes. Add the simple syrup and Sauternes. Shake well (while remembering that, after all, everything isn't always in a name).

3. Fill 2 highball or similarly sized glasses three-quarters full with ice cubes. Strain the mixture equally over the ice and then top off each glass with club soda. Stir gently.

4. Garnish each with a mint sprig and a remaining lime wedge and serve.

Quarter DECK

Serves 2

A few definitions. *Landlubber*, noun, 1: a person who lives on land; 2: a first-time or inexperienced sailor; 3: a generally boring person who doesn't think people should drink Quarter Decks in the backyard while sitting in a kiddy pool. *Pirate*, noun, 1: a person who robs at sea without regulation from a sovereign nation; 2: a person who can get away with wearing a floppy hat, some pants referred to as trousers, and large boots; 3: a person who may drink Quarter Decks in the backyard in a kiddy pool while saying things like "argh" and "ahoy, me hearties." Now, are you a landlubber or a pirate? I thought so.

Ice cubes

3 ounces dark rum

2 ounces mead

1 ounce fresh lime juice

2 lime slices for garnish

1. Fill a cocktail shaker halfway full with ice cubes. Add the rum, mead, and lime juice. Shake well while yelling out, "Weigh anchor! Hoist the mizzen."

2. Strain the mixture equally into 2 cocktail glasses or gilded goblets (depending on if your last raid included any gilded goblets). Garnish each with a lime slice and serve.

A NOTE: Mead is a wine relative traditionally made from honey, water, and yeast, sometimes referred to as "honey wine." And, for you trivia buffs, a brewery that only makes mead is called a meadery or a mazery. You may not have noticed, but it's available in most larger liquor stores and it can also be ordered online (try www.internetwines.com for a start).

A VARIATION: The Quarter Deck can also be made with sherry. I think if going this route you should call it the Eighth Deck and refer to yourself as "cabin boy." But I'm a particularly vicious pirate.

TUXEDO
Serves 2

Before you even ask, yes, you must wear a tuxedo when consuming these (this goes for both ladies and gentlemen, by the way). And yes, it should be of the ruffled lapel variety, or at least of the white-with-long-tail variety. And yes, there should be a type of dancing that might embarrass you later if someone happens to film it. And no, wearing a tuxedo T-shirt doesn't overwrite the above, except in really strenuous circumstances—like Friday after a long week of work, Saturday after a long afternoon of leaf-raking, or Sunday after a long morning of football-watching. But nothing else.

Ice cubes

3 ounces gin

1 ounce dry vermouth

1 ounce dry sherry (see A Note)

½ ounce maraschino liqueur

½ ounce Pernod

2 dashes Angostura bitters

1. Fill a cocktail shaker halfway full with ice cubes. Add everything—carefully, though, so you don't spill on your fancy duds. Shake well (also carefully of course).

2. Strain the Tux equally into 2 cocktail glasses and serve.

A NOTE: There are two main sherry types: fino and oloroso. Fino includes the manzanilla and amontillado varieties, which are used in this book. Olorosos tend to be aged longer and are richer in flavor and more expensive than the lighter, paler finos. All true sherries come from the Cadiz region around the town of Jerez, Spain.

A QUOTE: "The second property of your excellent sherris is the warming of the blood."

—William Shakespeare, *Henry IV, Part 2*

The Sake'd SAINT

Serves 2

This slightly holy drink is a variation on a cocktail I originally put together for the Tiger Tail (www.tigertailbar.com), a dandy spot in Seattle's Ballard neighborhood that has a tasty menu of Asian-inspired snacks and a swell selection of sake and beer, as well as some specialty cocktails that'll make you hum appreciatively. A warning, though: The menus change fairly regularly, so if you belly up to the Tiger Tail's lovely sorghum bar and ask for a Sake'd Saint (or something close to it), you may be disappointed—but I'll bet they'll serve you up another mix that'll make you just as happy.

4 star fruit slices	1. Combine 2 star fruit slices and the lemon wheels in a cocktail shaker. Using a muddler or a wooden tiger, muddle well.
2 lemon wheels	
Ice cubes	2. Fill the cocktail shaker halfway full with ice cubes. Add the sake, St-Germain, and apricot brandy. Shake extra well.
3 ounces Junmai or extra dry sake	
3 ounces St-Germain Elderflower Liqueur	3. Strain the mixture equally into 2 cocktail glasses. Garnish each with a remaining star fruit slice and serve.
½ ounce apricot brandy	

A NOTE: Star fruit (also known as coromandel gooseberry, kamranga, or five-finger fruit) is the fruit of the carambola tree and has a slightly tart taste as well as a striking star shape when sliced crosswise.

A SECOND NOTE: St-Germain is a liqueur made from French elderflower. There is only one word to describe its unique taste: amazing.

Sherry EGGNOG

Serves 2

I t's funny (in the "hmm" way, not the guffawing way) how drinks
change over time. Today, eggnog is a standard holiday party sta-
ple, one made with store-bought mixes and a little added alcohol,
or using a recipe that follows the basic creamy formula. This isn't a
bad deal, necessarily (well, using the store-bought mixes is bad,
because they don't taste one-sixteenth as good as homemade). But in
the 1941 book *Here's How: Mixed Drinks*, you'll find multiple options
for eggnog, including the following recipe, which doesn't have milk
products at all but which would make a scrumptious substitute at the
aforementioned holiday parties, as well as being a nice after-dinner
accompaniment at year-round affairs. So take a step back in time, and
take a step off the regular eggnog routine.

Ice cubes	**1.** Fill a cocktail shaker halfway full with ice cubes. Add the sherry, brandy, simple syrup, and eggs. Shake really well, for 10 to 15 seconds.
3 ounces man-zanilla sherry	
2 ounces brandy	**2.** Strain the mixture equally into 2 cocktail glasses, garnish each with ¼ teaspoon nutmeg, and serve.
2 ounces Simple Syrup (page 13)	
2 eggs	
½ teaspoon freshly grated nutmeg for garnish	

A NOTE: As this recipe uses raw eggs, don't serve it to the elderly or anyone
with a compromised immune system.

MEASUREMENT *Equivalents*

Please note that all conversions are approximate.

LIQUID CONVERSIONS

U.S.	IMPERIAL	METRIC
1 tsp	—	5 ml
1 tbs	½ fl oz	15 ml
2 tbs	1 fl oz	30 ml
3 tbs	1½ fl oz	45 ml
¼ cup	2 fl oz	60 ml
⅓ cup	2½ fl oz	75 ml
⅓ cup + 1 tbs	3 fl oz	90 ml
⅓ cup + 2 tbs	3½ fl oz	100 ml
½ cup	4 fl oz	120 ml
⅓ cup	5 fl oz	150 ml
¾ cup	6 fl oz	180 ml
¾ cup + 2 tbs	7 fl oz	200 ml
1 cup	8 fl oz	240 ml
1 cup + 2 tbs	9 fl oz	275 ml
1¼ cups	10 fl oz	300 ml
1⅓ cups	11 fl oz	325 ml
1½ cups	12 fl oz	350 ml
1⅔ cups	13 fl oz	375 ml
1¾ cups	14 fl oz	400 ml
1¾ cups + 2 tbs	15 fl oz	450 ml
2 cups (1 pint)	16 fl oz	475 ml
2½ cups	20 fl oz	600 ml
3 cups	24 fl oz	720 ml
4 cups (1 quart)	32 fl oz	945 ml

(1,000 ml is 1 liter)

INDEX